To access the free online q▮ activities for the Global Reg▮ visit us online at

www.globalregentsreview.com

and click on the tab that says

Global Regents Quizzes and Activities

If requested, enter password:

globalregents

(Enter without spaces between the words.)

Please use these quizzes and activities to test and reinforce your knowledge.

Dedication:

This book is dedicated to all of the students who need to do well on the Global History Regents Exam. This can be a challenging test. If you have failed this test before, you probably lack confidence in yourself, but if you work hard and learn the main ideas in this book, you will succeed. Teachers can use this book for summary or review lessons. This is not a textbook for the subject, it's the best book for the test, because all it contains is all any student would really have to know to master the multiple choice portion of the exam. Any student that demolishes the multiple choice has a great chance of getting a high grade on the exam. So, let's go to work and have some fun while we're learning.

Working for Your Success,

Mr. Vieira

Principal of ScholarSkills

How to use this book

This book works if you work. There are no easy ways to succeed. Effort leads to excellence. This is the second ebook. The first one is the Book of Main Idea Charts. These books should be used together. Keep the Main Idea Chart physical or digital version open whenever you are attempting any regents questions. This will help you to use the information on those charts to answer the questions on your quiz or test.

How to use your Main Idea Charts, Learning Activities and Quizzes

Step one:
Read the main idea at the top of the Chart page, and write that main idea into your notes.

Step two:
Read the chart with the boxes below the main idea, and write each piece of information in those boxes on separate lines in your notes.

Step three:
If you are using the physical book, download a QR scanner and scan the code on the last page of the book. This will take you to your class page where you will see information about each topic in the following order:

Quizzes
Learning games
Links to the main idea charts online

If you are using the e-book, then simply click on the Activities link and find the activities for the topic that you are studying. Activities are listed in alphabetical order.

Step four:
Play the Learning Games:
Examples: Rags to Riches
Hangman
Matching

Step five:
Take the quiz as many times as you need to get every question correct. Keep referring to your Main Idea Chart as you answer the questions. This will help you to gain the confidence you need.

Step six:
Start a regents topic notebook. Use regents questions to find and record more information about each regent topic. Write down every answer from each regents question about that topic. Write down any phrase or word in the question that gives you a clue or more information about the topic. Your goal is to become completely familiar with every type of question and answer about the topics that are consistently repeated on each exam. Set aside at least three pages for each topic.

Sample notebook format:

Question:
The Indus and Huang He (Yellow) rivers are both closely associated with

(1) border disputes
(2) sacred biblical sites
(3) cradles of early civilization
(4) oil discoveries

Topic:
This question is about Indus and Huang He rivers

Main Idea: (from chart or other information)

All questions about this topic contain the idea that:

Early civilizations grew up around river valleys which were a source of irrigation and transportation.

Key words and connections from the chart and regents questions:
All questions or correct answers about this topic contain one or more of these key words or phrases:

Early civilizations, rivers, river valleys,

Notes and other information about the topic:

Most of the questions that deal with rivers and river valleys are about ancient civilizations that grew up around the Tigris and Euphrates rivers in Mesopotamia, the Indus river in India, the Nile river in Egypt, and the Yellow river or Huang He in China.

Table of Contents

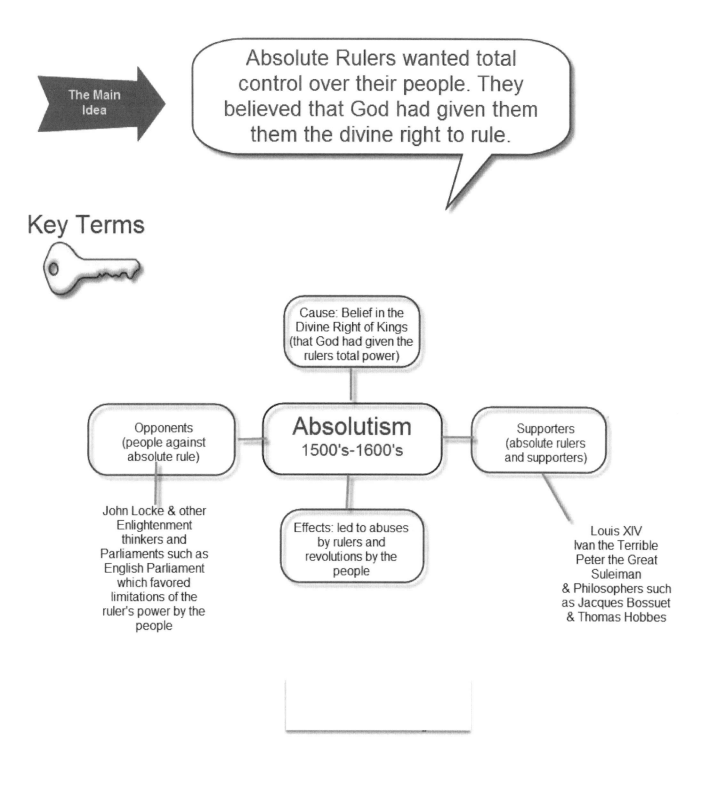

The Main Idea

Absolute Rulers wanted total control over their people. They believed that God had given them them the divine right to rule.

Key Terms

Cause: Belief in the Divine Right of Kings (that God had given the rulers total power)

Opponents (people against absolute rule)

Absolutism
1500's-1600's

Supporters (absolute rulers and supporters)

John Locke & other Enlightenment thinkers and Parliaments such as English Parliament which favored limitations of the ruler's power by the people

Effects: led to abuses by rulers and revolutions by the people

Louis XIV
Ivan the Terrible
Peter the Great
Suleiman
& Philosophers such as Jacques Bossuet & Thomas Hobbes

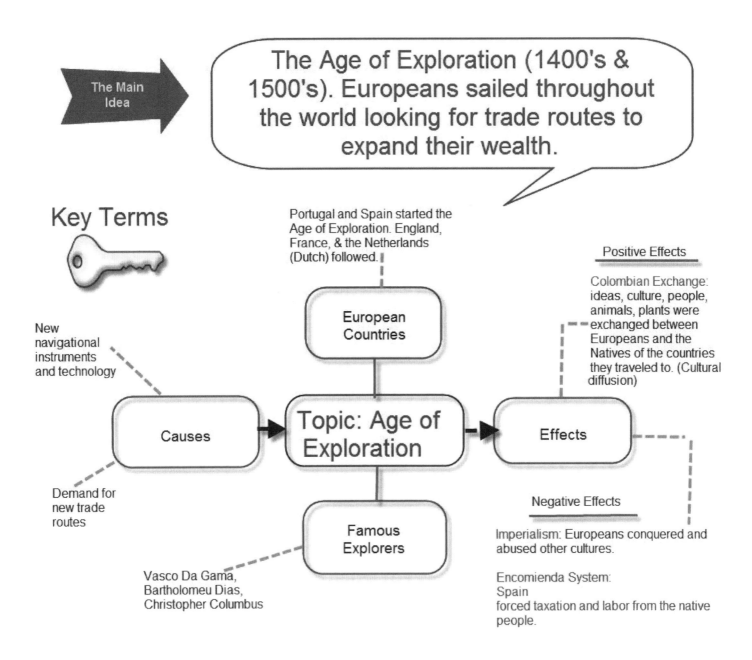

The Main Idea

The Age of Exploration (1400's & 1500's). Europeans sailed throughout the world looking for trade routes to expand their wealth.

Key Terms

Portugal and Spain started the Age of Exploration. England, France, & the Netherlands (Dutch) followed.

New navigational instruments and technology

Demand for new trade routes

Causes

European Countries

Topic: Age of Exploration

Famous Explorers

Vasco Da Gama, Bartholomeu Dias, Christopher Columbus

Effects

Positive Effects

Colombian Exchange: ideas, culture, people, animals, plants were exchanged between Europeans and the Natives of the countries they traveled to. (Cultural diffusion)

Negative Effects

Imperialism: Europeans conquered and abused other cultures.

Encomienda System: Spain forced taxation and labor from the native people.

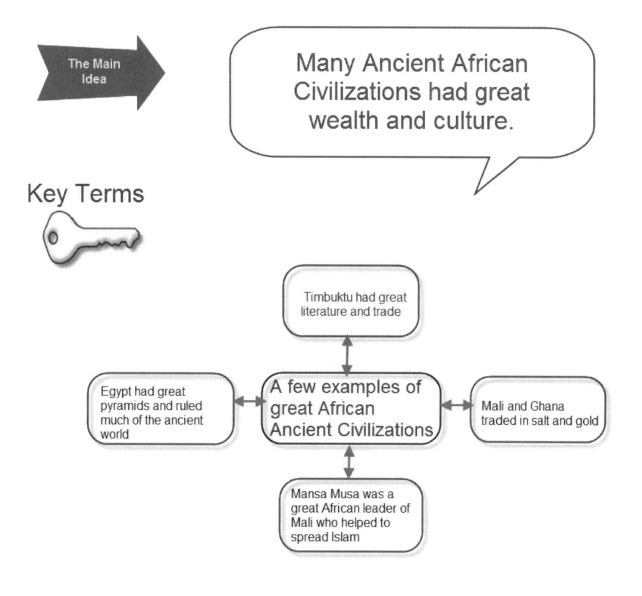

The Main Idea

Many Ancient African Civilizations had great wealth and culture.

Key Terms

Timbuktu had great literature and trade

Egypt had great pyramids and ruled much of the ancient world

A few examples of great African Ancient Civilizations

Mali and Ghana traded in salt and gold

Mansa Musa was a great African leader of Mali who helped to spread Islam

The Main Idea

Ancient Civilizations developed in river valleys because the rivers made the soil fertile for farming

Key Terms

Great Rivers

Huang He, Indus, Nile, Tigris & Euphrates

Reason for location

River Valleys provided fertile soil and means for transportation

Topic

Ancient Civilizations

Early Civilizations

Sumer, Indus Valley, Egypt, China

Key Ideas

Geography has a great effect on civilization

The Main Idea

Apartheid was the system of segregation in South Africa used by Whites to control the majority Black **Population**

Key Terms

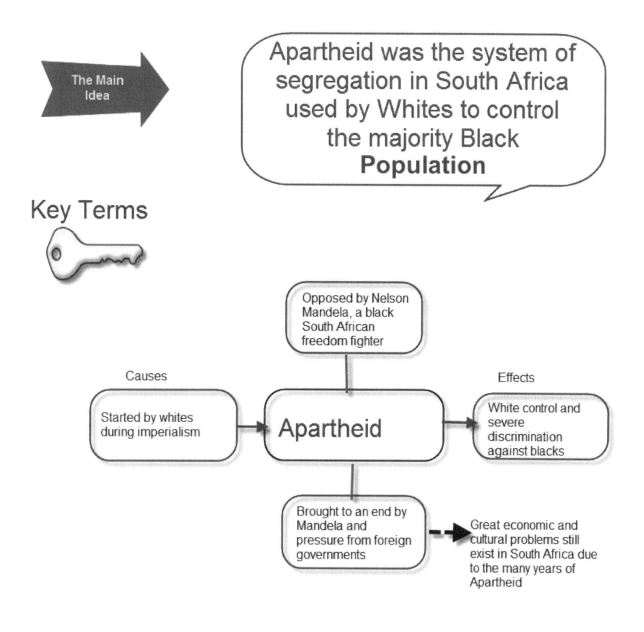

Opposed by Nelson Mandela, a black South African freedom fighter

Causes

Started by whites during imperialism

Apartheid

Effects

White control and severe discrimination against blacks

Brought to an end by Mandela and pressure from foreign governments

Great economic and cultural problems still exist in South Africa due to the many years of Apartheid

The Main Idea

Mustafa Kemal Ataturk tried to westernize Turkey in the 1920's and 1930's.

Key Terms

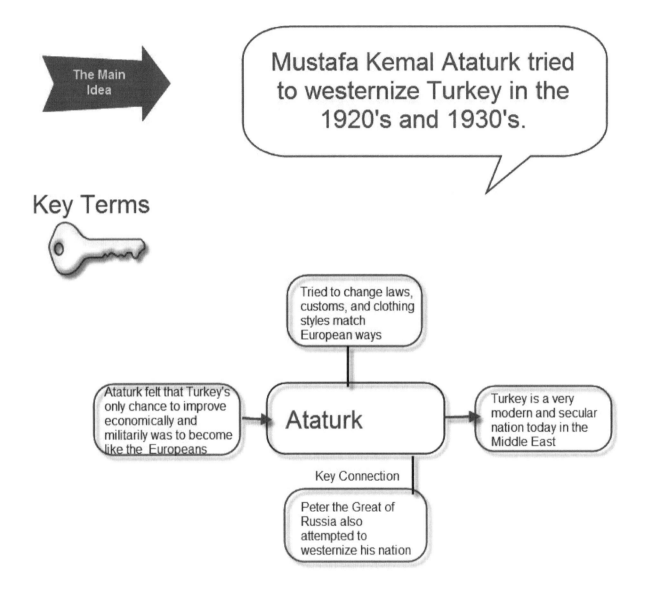

Tried to change laws, customs, and clothing styles match European ways

Ataturk felt that Turkey's only chance to improve economically and militarily was to become like the Europeans

Ataturk

Turkey is a very modern and secular nation today in the Middle East

Key Connection

Peter the Great of Russia also attempted to westernize his nation

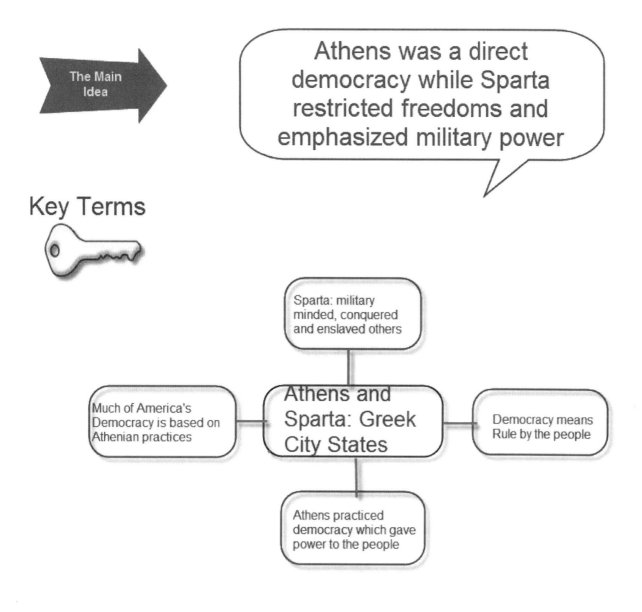

The Main Idea

Athens was a direct democracy while Sparta restricted freedoms and emphasized military power

Key Terms

Sparta: military minded, conquered and enslaved others

Much of America's Democracy is based on Athenian practices

Athens and Sparta: Greek City States

Democracy means Rule by the people

Athens practiced democracy which gave power to the people

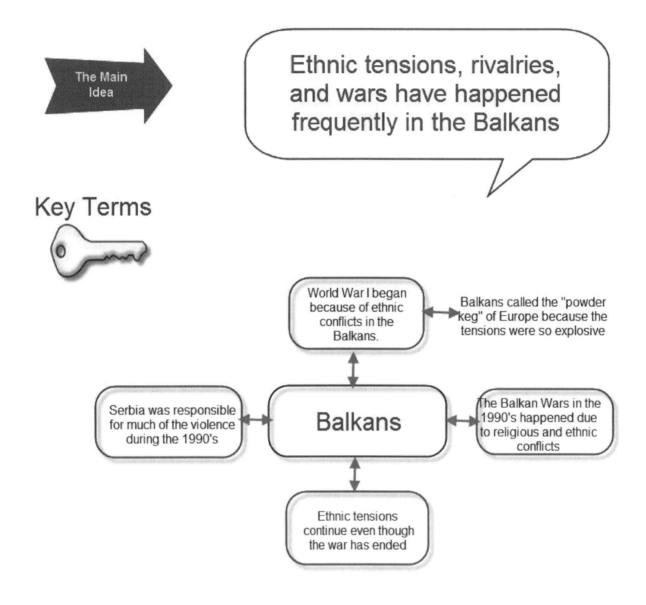

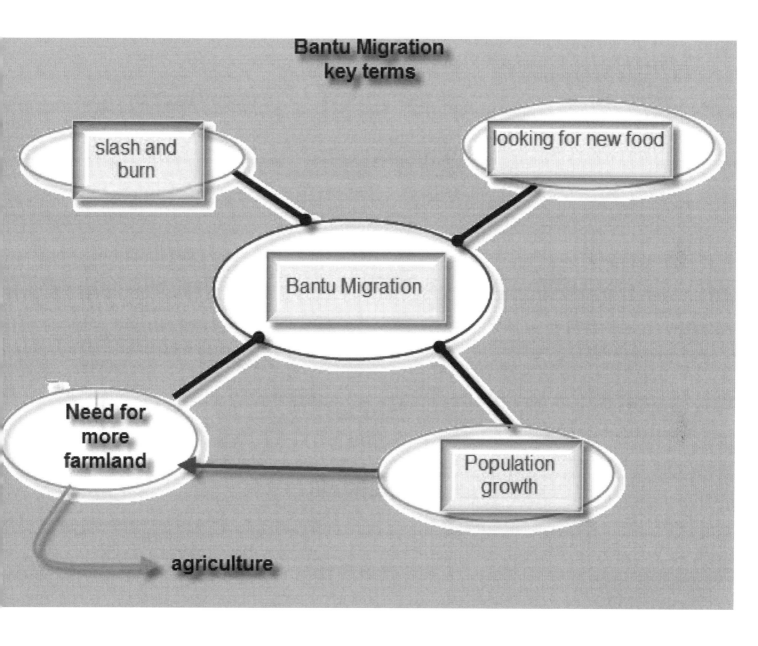

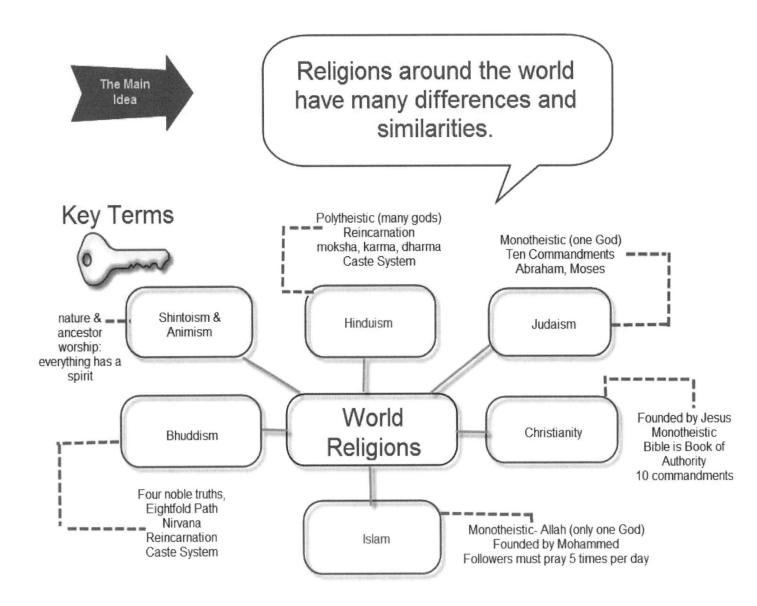

The Main Idea

Religions around the world have many differences and similarities.

Key Terms

Polytheistic (many gods)
Reincarnation
moksha, karma, dharma
Caste System

Monotheistic (one God)
Ten Commandments
Abraham, Moses

nature & ancestor worship: everything has a spirit

Shintoism & Animism

Hinduism

Judaism

Bhuddism

World Religions

Christianity

Founded by Jesus
Monotheistic
Bible is Book of Authority
10 commandments

Four noble truths,
Eightfold Path
Nirvana
Reincarnation
Caste System

Islam

Monotheistic- Allah (only one God)
Founded by Mohammed
Followers must pray 5 times per day

The Main Idea

The Black Death (or Bubonic Plague) was a terrible disease that was spread from Central Asia throughout Europe and the Mediterranean by trade and

Key Terms

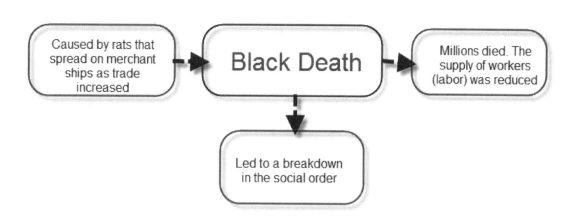

Caused by rats that spread on merchant ships as trade increased → **Black Death** → Millions died. The supply of workers (labor) was reduced

Led to a breakdown in the social order

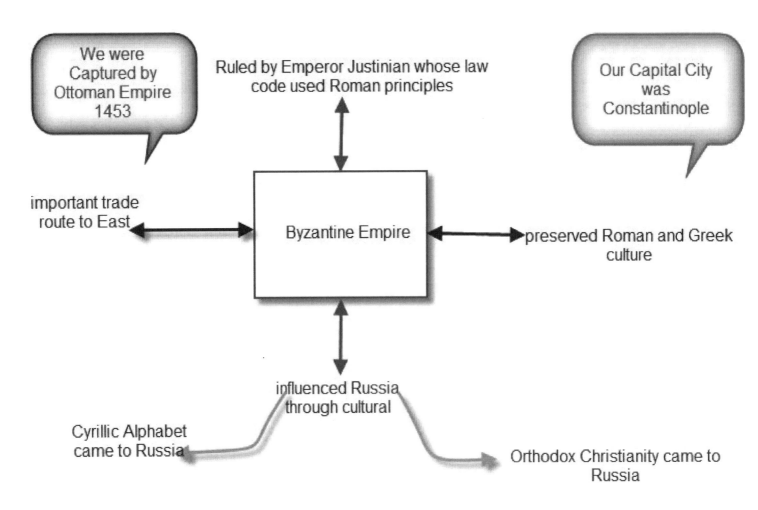

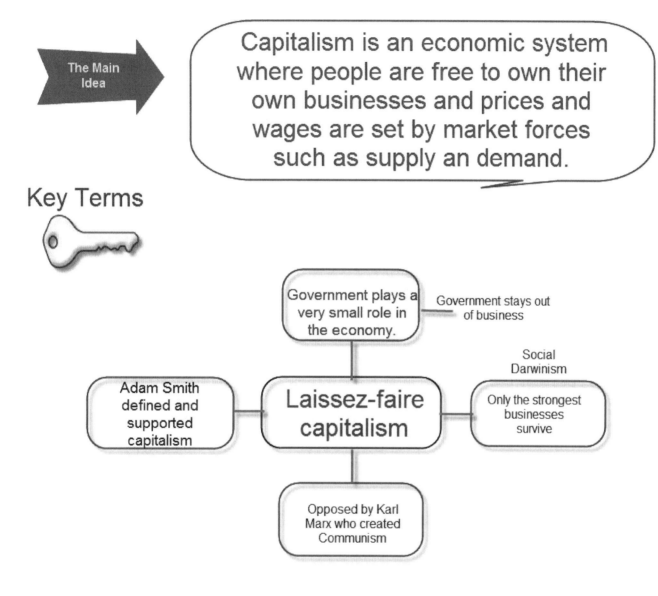

The Main Idea

Capitalism is an economic system where people are free to own their own businesses and prices and wages are set by market forces such as supply an demand.

Key Terms

Government plays a very small role in the economy.

Government stays out of business

Adam Smith defined and supported capitalism

Laissez-faire capitalism

Social Darwinism

Only the strongest businesses survive

Opposed by Karl Marx who created Communism

The Main Idea

The Caste System is a social structure where people are separated from each other and ranked forever below or above each other based on the family and class they were born into.

Key Terms

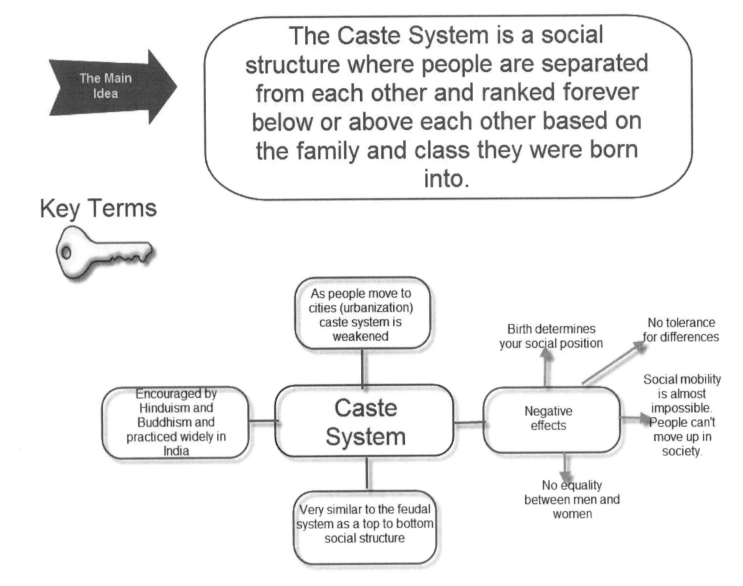

As people move to cities (urbanization) caste system is weakened

Birth determines your social position

No tolerance for differences

Encouraged by Hinduism and Buddhism and practiced widely in India

Caste System

Negative effects

Social mobility is almost impossible. People can't move up in society.

Very similar to the feudal system as a top to bottom social structure

No equality between men and women

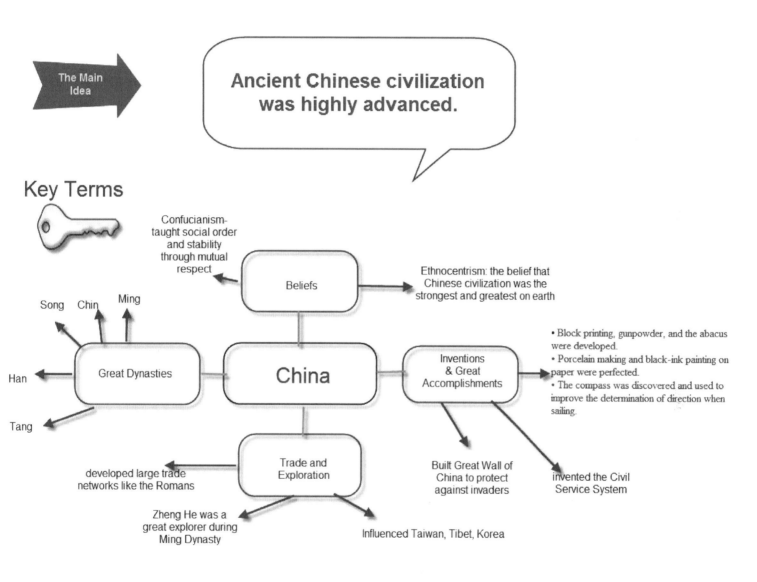

The Main Idea

Ancient Chinese civilization was highly advanced.

Key Terms

Confucianism- taught social order and stability through mutual respect

Ethnocentrism: the belief that Chinese civilization was the strongest and greatest on earth

Beliefs

Song   Chin   Ming

Han

Great Dynasties

China

Inventions & Great Accomplishments

• Block printing, gunpowder, and the abacus were developed.
• Porcelain making and black-ink painting on paper were perfected.
• The compass was discovered and used to improve the determination of direction when sailing.

Tang

Trade and Exploration

developed large trade networks like the Romans

Zheng He was a great explorer during Ming Dynasty

Influenced Taiwan, Tibet, Korea

Built Great Wall of China to protect against invaders

invented the Civil Service System

The Main
Idea

The Cold War was the conflict between the U.S. and the Soviet Union which led to violent conflicts throughout the world from the end of World War II to the collapse of the Soviet Union in 1991.

Key Terms

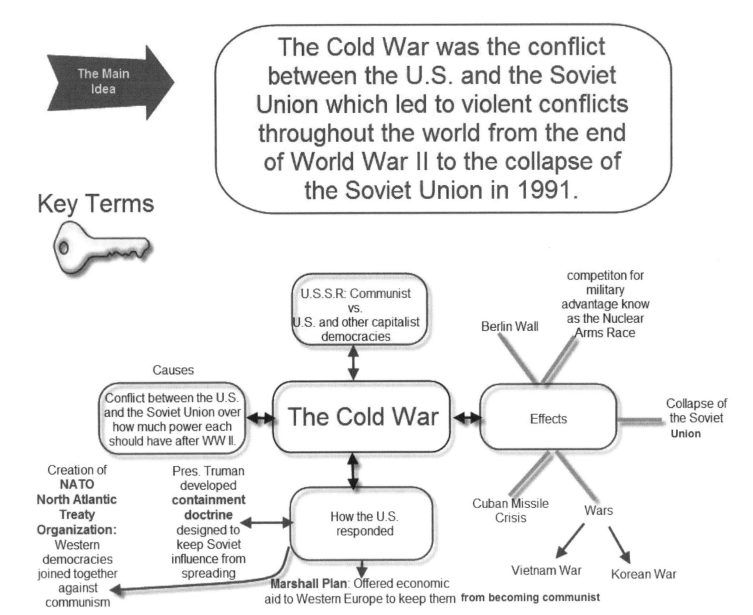

U.S.S.R: Communist
vs.
U.S. and other capitalist
democracies

competiton for
military
advantage know
as the Nuclear
Arms Race

Berlin Wall

Causes

Conflict between the U.S. and the Soviet Union over how much power each should have after WW II.

The Cold War

Effects

Collapse of
the Soviet
Union

Creation of
NATO
North Atlantic
Treaty
Organization:
Western
democracies
joined together
against
communism

Pres. Truman
developed
containment
doctrine
designed to
keep Soviet
influence from
spreading

How the U.S.
responded

Cuban Missile
Crisis

Wars

Vietnam War   Korean War

Marshall Plan: Offered economic
aid to Western Europe to keep them **from becoming communist**

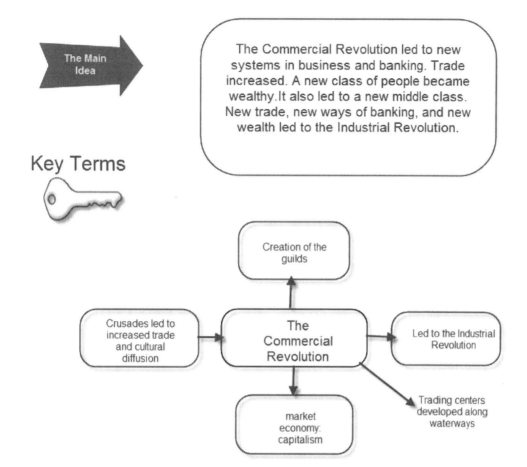

The Main Idea

The Commercial Revolution led to new systems in business and banking. Trade increased. A new class of people became wealthy. It also led to a new middle class. New trade, new ways of banking, and new wealth led to the Industrial Revolution.

Key Terms

Creation of the guilds

Crusades led to increased trade and cultural diffusion

The Commercial Revolution

Led to the Industrial Revolution

market economy: capitalism

Trading centers developed along waterways

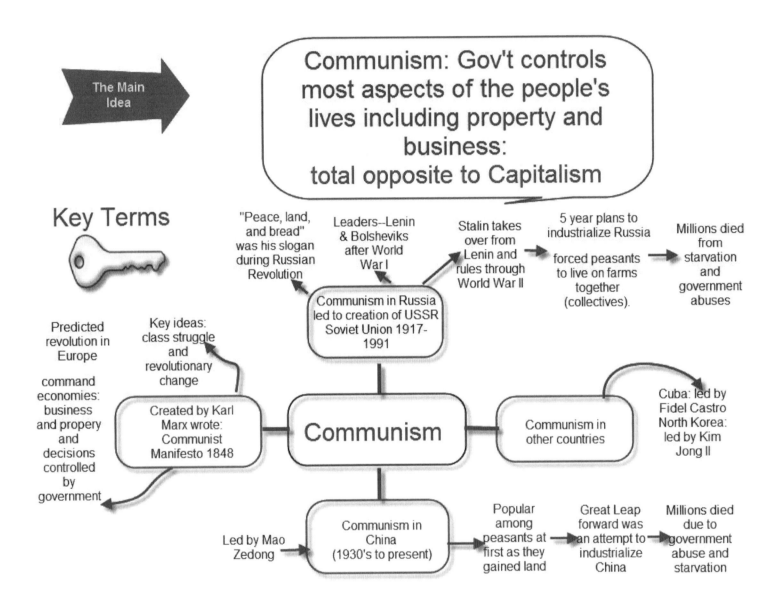

The Main Idea

Communism: Gov't controls most aspects of the people's lives including property and business:
total opposite to Capitalism

Key Terms

"Peace, land, and bread" was his slogan during Russian Revolution

Leaders--Lenin & Bolsheviks after World War I

Stalin takes over from Lenin and rules through World War II

5 year plans to industrialize Russia

forced peasants to live on farms together (collectives).

Millions died from starvation and government abuses

Communism in Russia led to creation of USSR Soviet Union 1917-1991

Predicted revolution in Europe

Key ideas: class struggle and revolutionary change

command economies: business and propery and decisions controlled by government

Created by Karl Marx wrote: Communist Manifesto 1848

Communism

Communism in other countries

Cuba: led by Fidel Castro North Korea: led by Kim Jong II

Led by Mao Zedong

Communism in China (1930's to present)

Popular among peasants at first as they gained land

Great Leap forward was an attempt to industrialize China

Millions died due to government abuse and starvation

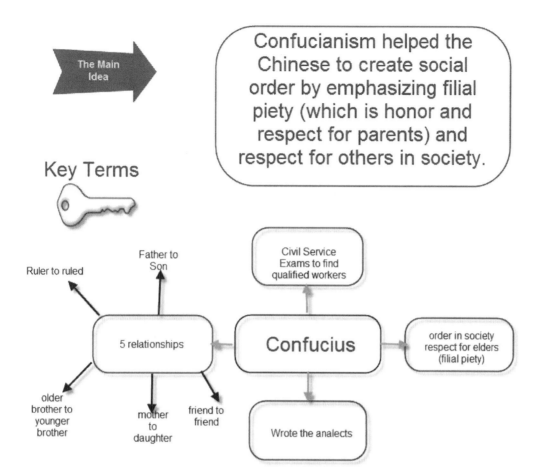

The Main Idea

Confucianism helped the Chinese to create social order by emphasizing filial piety (which is honor and respect for parents) and respect for others in society.

Key Terms

Ruler to ruled

Father to Son

Civil Service Exams to find qualified workers

5 relationships

Confucius

order in society respect for elders (filial piety)

older brother to younger brother

mother to daughter

friend to friend

Wrote the analects

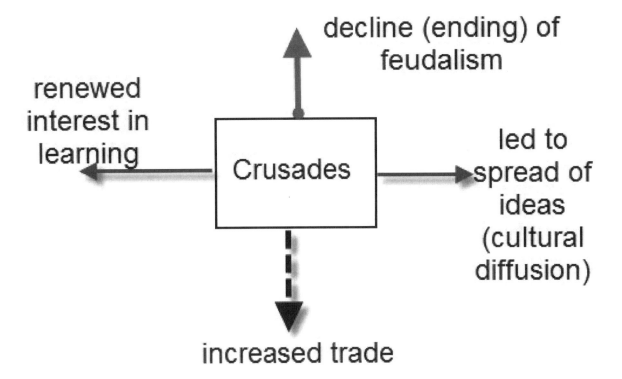

The Main Idea

Cultural diffusion is the spread of ideas and culture through travel, trade, and human interaction.

Key Terms

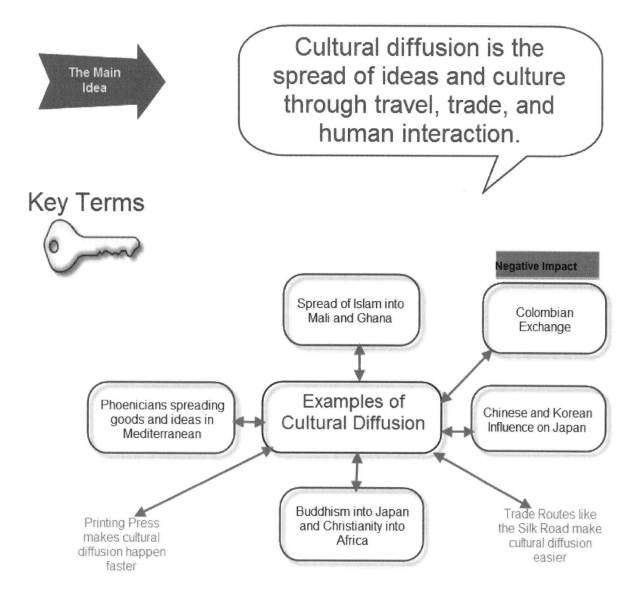

Spread of Islam into Mali and Ghana

Negative Impact

Colombian Exchange

Phoenicians spreading goods and ideas in Mediterranean

Examples of Cultural Diffusion

Chinese and Korean Influence on Japan

Printing Press makes cultural diffusion happen faster

Buddhism into Japan and Christianity into Africa

Trade Routes like the Silk Road make cultural diffusion easier

The Main Idea

Enlightenment thinkers believed that human reason would lead to progress and that the power of rulers should be limited so that the people's rights could be protected.

Key Terms

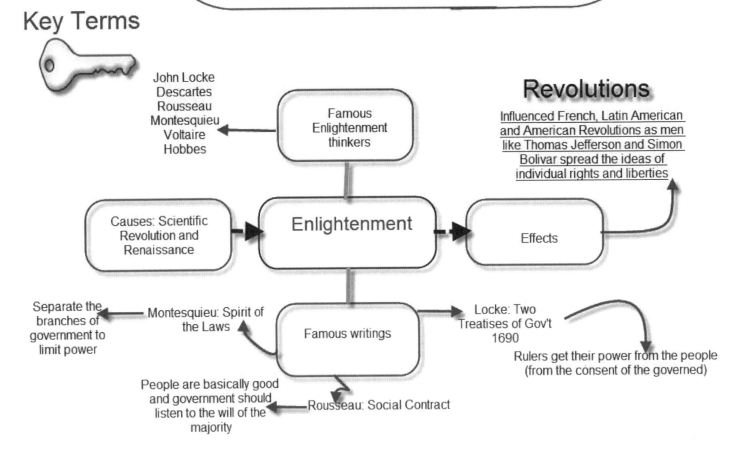

John Locke
Descartes
Rousseau
Montesquieu
Voltaire
Hobbes

Famous Enlightenment thinkers

Revolutions

Influenced French, Latin American and American Revolutions as men like Thomas Jefferson and Simon Bolivar spread the ideas of individual rights and liberties

Causes: Scientific Revolution and Renaissance

Enlightenment

Effects

Separate the branches of government to limit power

Montesquieu: Spirit of the Laws

Famous writings

Locke: Two Treatises of Gov't 1690

Rulers get their power from the people (from the consent of the governed)

People are basically good and government should listen to the will of the majority

Rousseau: Social Contract

22

The Main Idea

Environmental problems such as deforestation, pollution, and global warming are a threat to the whole earth.

Key Terms

Many species of animals are destroyed; global warming; soil erosion

Deforestation: destruction of rain forests especially in Amazon Basin

Excuses for destroying forests:

Will help the economy and the people through cattle raising, farming, and mining in the rain forests

Pollution and Acid rain

Environmental Problems

Global warming: depletion of ozone

Key theme: Human beings and technology can have negative effects on the environment

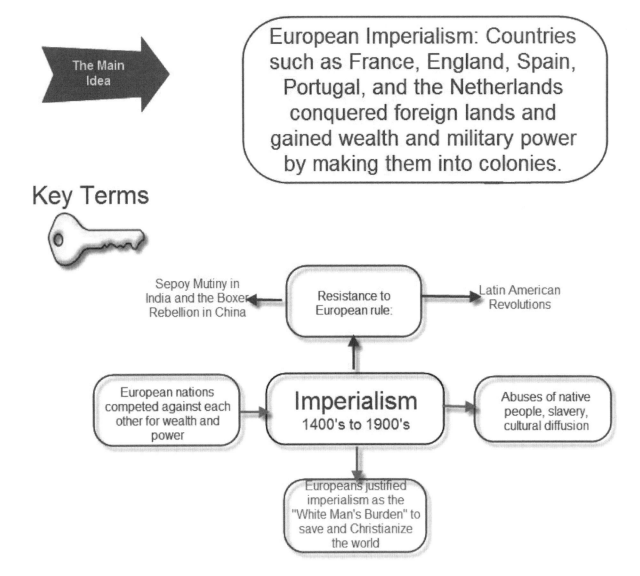

The Main Idea

European Imperialism: Countries such as France, England, Spain, Portugal, and the Netherlands conquered foreign lands and gained wealth and military power by making them into colonies.

Key Terms

Sepoy Mutiny in India and the Boxer Rebellion in China

Resistance to European rule:

Latin American Revolutions

European nations competed against each other for wealth and power

Imperialism 1400's to 1900's

Abuses of native people, slavery, cultural diffusion

Europeans justified imperialism as the "White Man's Burden" to save and Christianize the world

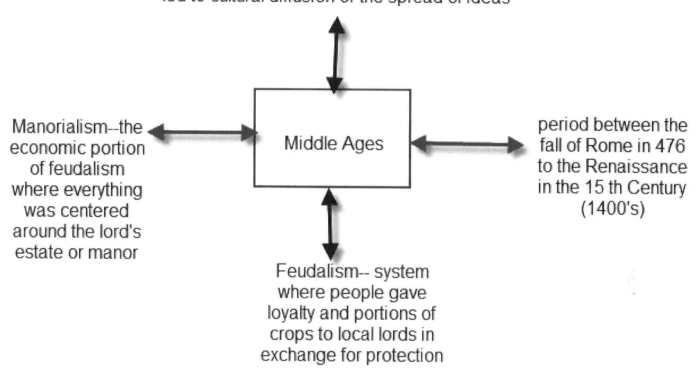

Crusades--wars between Christians and Muslims
led to cultural diffusion or the spread of ideas

Manorialism--the
economic portion
of feudalism
where everything
was centered
around the lord's
estate or manor

Middle Ages

period between the
fall of Rome in 476
to the Renaissance
in the 15 th Century
(1400's)

Feudalism-- system
where people gave
loyalty and portions of
crops to local lords in
exchange for protection

The Main Idea

French Revolution:(1789-1799) period of radical change in France when absolute monarchy was overthrown in favor of individual rights and a limited constitutional government. But terror and executions reigned as different groups competed for power.

Key Terms

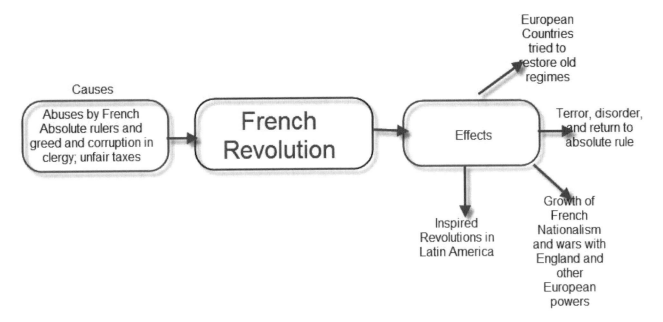

Causes

Abuses by French Absolute rulers and greed and corruption in clergy; unfair taxes

French Revolution

Effects

European Countries tried to restore old regimes

Terror, disorder, and return to absolute rule

Growth of French Nationalism and wars with England and other European powers

Inspired Revolutions in Latin America

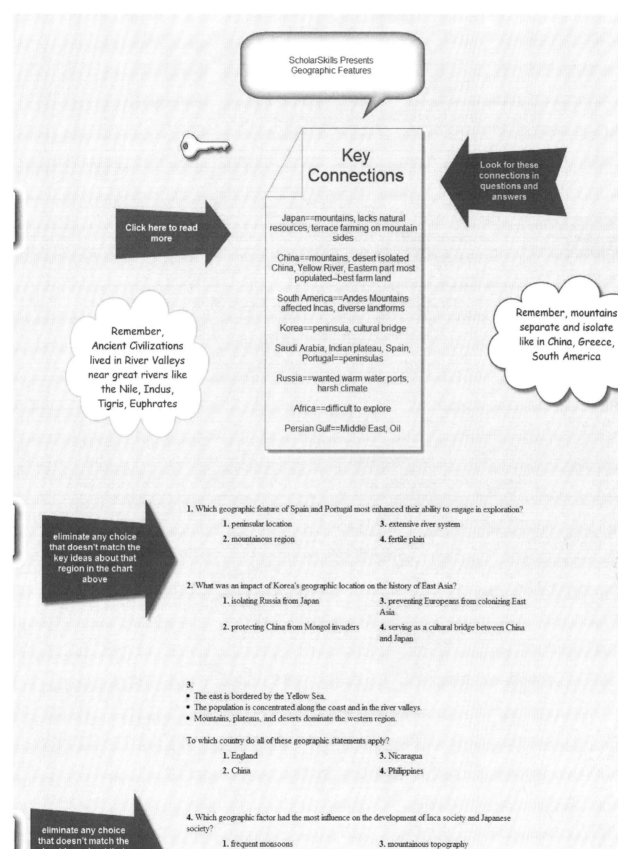

ScholarSkills Presents
Geographic Features

Key Connections

Japan==mountains, lacks natural resources, terrace farming on mountain sides

China==mountains, desert isolated China, Yellow River, Eastern part most populated--best farm land

South America==Andes Mountains affected Incas, diverse landforms

Korea==peninsula, cultural bridge

Saudi Arabia, Indian plateau, Spain, Portugal==peninsulas

Russia==wanted warm water ports, harsh climate

Africa==difficult to explore

Persian Gulf==Middle East, Oil

Look for these connections in questions and answers

Click here to read more

Remember, Ancient Civilizations lived in River Valleys near great rivers like the Nile, Indus, Tigris, Euphrates

Remember, mountains separate and isolate like in China, Greece, South America

eliminate any choice that doesn't match the key ideas about that region in the chart above

1. Which geographic feature of Spain and Portugal most enhanced their ability to engage in exploration?

1. peninsular location
2. mountainous region
3. extensive river system
4. fertile plain

2. What was an impact of Korea's geographic location on the history of East Asia?

1. isolating Russia from Japan
2. protecting China from Mongol invaders
3. preventing Europeans from colonizing East Asia
4. serving as a cultural bridge between China and Japan

3.
• The east is bordered by the Yellow Sea.
• The population is concentrated along the coast and in the river valleys.
• Mountains, plateaus, and deserts dominate the western region.

To which country do all of these geographic statements apply?

1. England
2. China
3. Nicaragua
4. Philippines

eliminate any choice that doesn't match the key ideas about that region in the chart above

4. Which geographic factor had the most influence on the development of Inca society and Japanese society?

1. frequent monsoons
2. large deserts
3. mountainous topography
4. tropical climate

5.

27

The Main Idea

The Glorious Revolution: In 1688, the Parliament of England overthrew King James II and placed William of Orange into Power. This marked the end of Absolute Rule and the Divine Right of Kings in England.

Key Terms

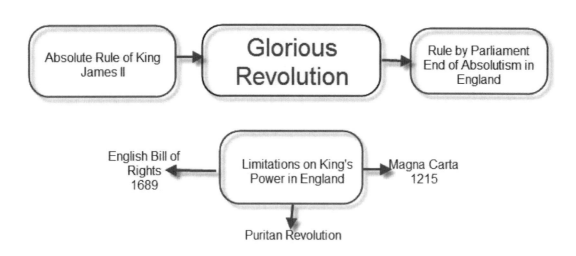

Absolute Rule of King James II → Glorious Revolution → Rule by Parliament End of Absolutism in England

English Bill of Rights 1689 ← Limitations on King's Power in England → Magna Carta 1215

Puritan Revolution

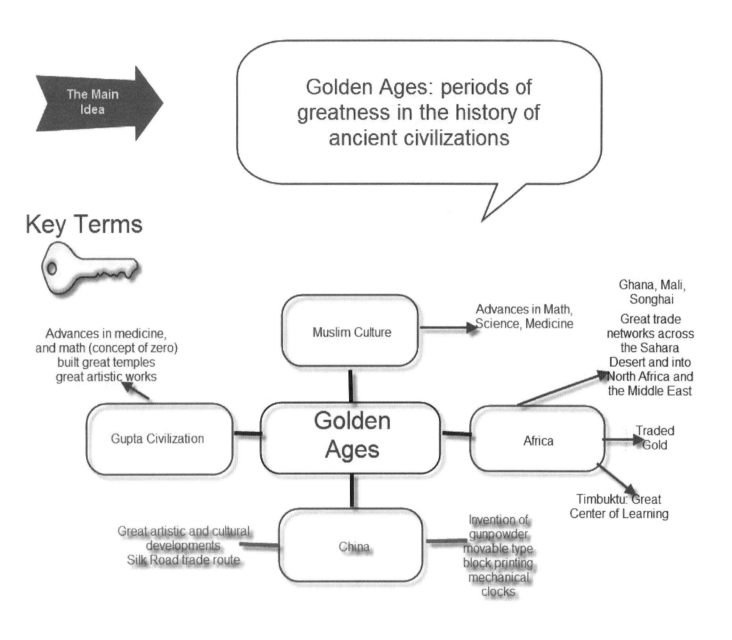

The Main Idea

Golden Ages: periods of greatness in the history of ancient civilizations

Key Terms

Muslim Culture → Advances in Math, Science, Medicine

Ghana, Mali, Songhai

Great trade networks across the Sahara Desert and into North Africa and the Middle East

Advances in medicine, and math (concept of zero) built great temples great artistic works

Gupta Civilization

Golden Ages

Africa → Traded Gold

Timbuktu: Great Center of Learning

Great artistic and cultural developments
Silk Road trade route

China

Invention of gunpowder movable type block printing mechanical clocks

Gorbachev: Leader of the Soviet Union whose economic and political reforms in the 1980's led to the fall of communism

Key Terms

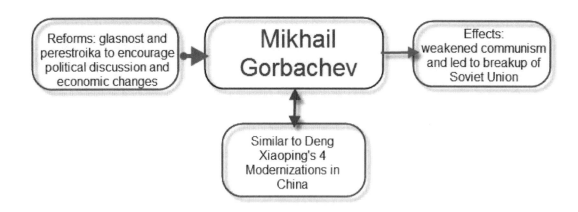

Reforms: glasnost and perestroika to encourage political discussion and economic changes

Mikhail Gorbachev

Effects: weakened communism and led to breakup of Soviet Union

Similar to Deng Xiaoping's 4 Modernizations in China

The Main Idea

The Green Revolution: technological advances in agriculture that increased the food supply in many developing nations.

Key Terms

| Technological advances in agriculture | → | **Green Revolution** | → | Prevented famine in many countries such as India |

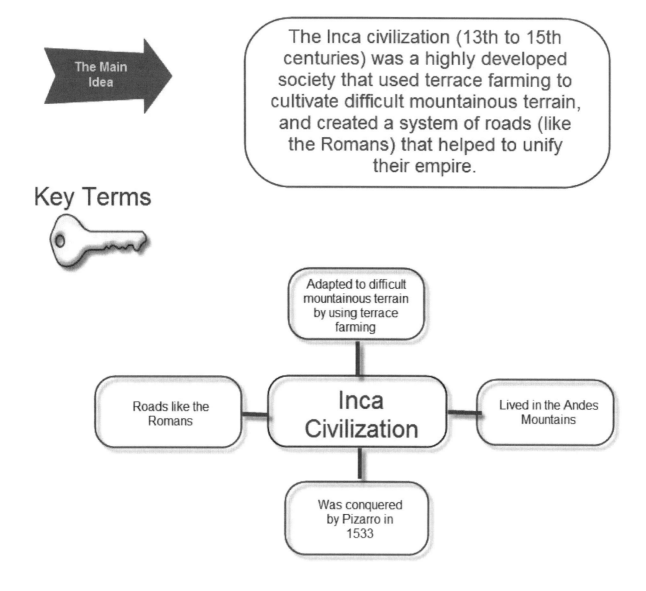

The Main Idea

The Inca civilization (13th to 15th centuries) was a highly developed society that used terrace farming to cultivate difficult mountainous terrain, and created a system of roads (like the Romans) that helped to unify their empire.

Key Terms

Adapted to difficult mountainous terrain by using terrace farming

Roads like the Romans

Inca Civilization

Lived in the Andes Mountains

Was conquered by Pizarro in 1533

Key ideas:
Industrial Revolution led to
a better standard of living for many people, but it also led to bad working conditions and terrible treatment of workers. This led to Karl Marx's writings about Communism. Marx blamed Capitalism for society's problems.

ScholarSkills Presents:
The Industrial Revolution

The Industrial Revolution created positive and negative changes

Key Terms

Karl Marx-Communism

England--many natural resources

Growth of towns, cities, urban areas

Capitalism--Europe, U.S. economic system

Communism--opposes Capitalism

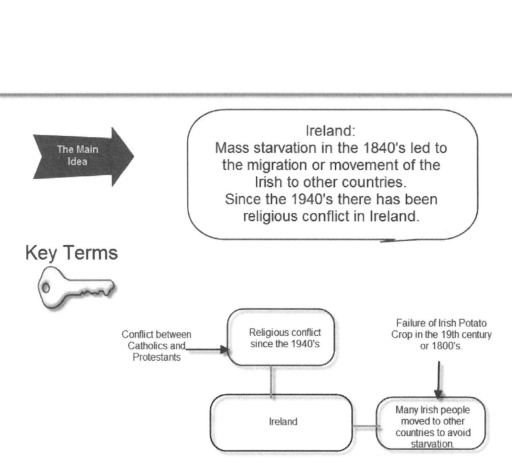

The Main Idea

Ireland:
Mass starvation in the 1840's led to the migration or movement of the Irish to other countries.
Since the 1940's there has been religious conflict in Ireland.

Key Terms

Conflict between Catholics and Protestants

Religious conflict since the 1940's

Failure of Irish Potato Crop in the 19th century or 1800's.

Ireland

Many Irish people moved to other countries to avoid starvation.

The Main Idea

Latin American revolutionaries, influenced by the Enlightenment and the French and American Revolutions, rebelled against European rule in the 18th and 19th centuries.

Key Terms

Influenced by the Englightenment and French Revolution ideas of liberty and rights for all → Latin American Revolutionaries → Simon Bolivar Jose de San Martin Toussaint L' Ouverture

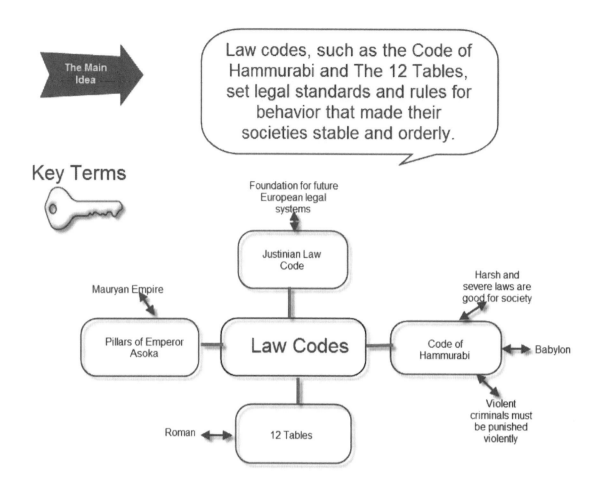

The Main Idea

Law codes, such as the Code of Hammurabi and The 12 Tables, set legal standards and rules for behavior that made their societies stable and orderly.

Key Terms

Foundation for future European legal systems

Justinian Law Code

Mauryan Empire

Pillars of Emperor Asoka

Law Codes

Code of Hammurabi

Harsh and severe laws are good for society

Babylon

Violent criminals must be punished violently

Roman

12 Tables

The Main Idea

> The League of Nations was designed to prevent wars such as World War I from ever happening again. It did not work.

Key Terms

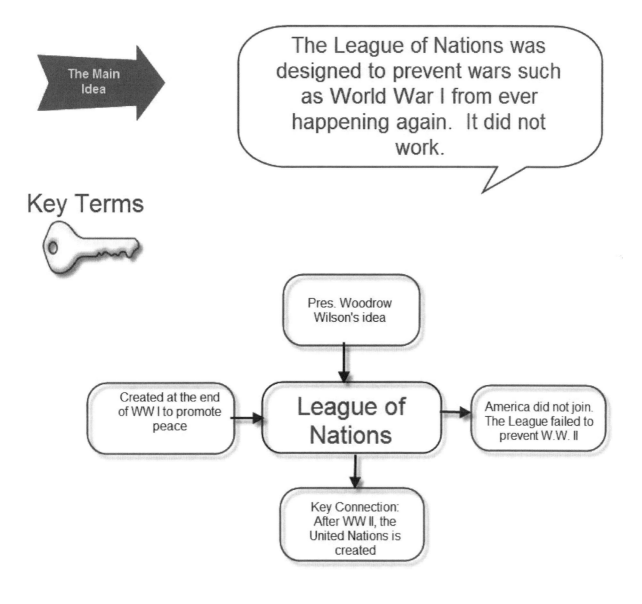

Pres. Woodrow Wilson's idea

Created at the end of WW I to promote peace

League of Nations

America did not join. The League failed to prevent W.W. II

Key Connection: After WW II, the United Nations is created

The Main Idea

The Magna Carta (1215): A list of feudal rights during the Middle Ages that limited the power of the King.

Key Terms

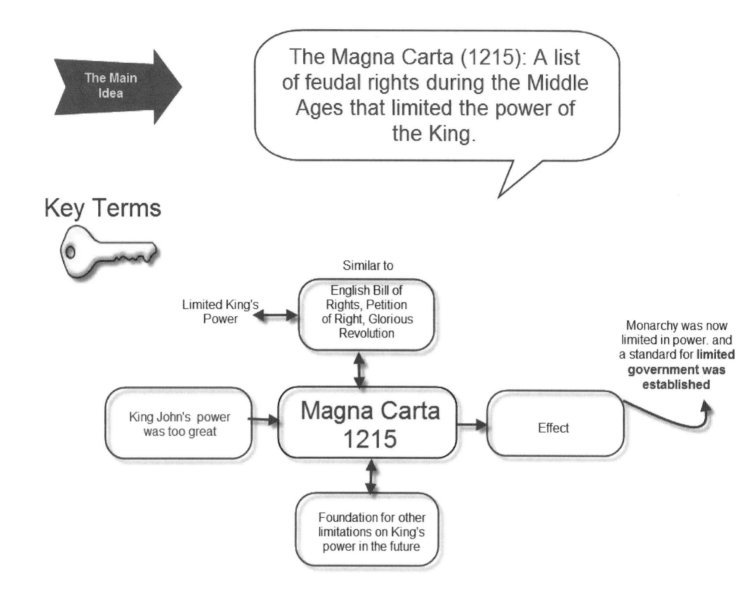

Similar to

English Bill of Rights, Petition of Right, Glorious Revolution

Limited King's Power

Monarchy was now limited in power. and a standard for **limited government was established**

King John's power was too great

Magna Carta 1215

Effect

Foundation for other limitations on King's power in the future

The Main Idea

> Mansa Musa was the great ruler of Mali. He used the wealth and power that he obtained from the gold for salt trade to spread Islamic learning and culture.

Key Terms

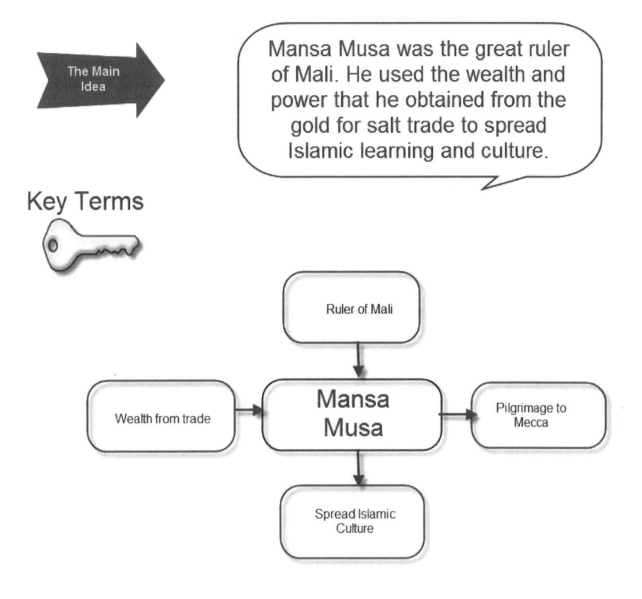

Ruler of Mali

Wealth from trade → **Mansa Musa** → Pilgrimage to Mecca

Spread Islamic Culture

The Main Idea

Marco Polo: an Italian explorer in the 13th century (1200's) whose travels and writings opened up European trade with Central Asia and China along the Silk Road trade route.

Key Terms

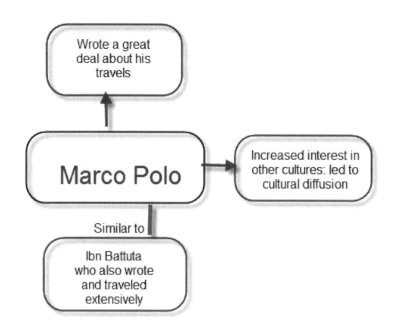

Wrote a great deal about his travels

Marco Polo

Increased interest in other cultures: led to cultural diffusion

Similar to

Ibn Battuta who also wrote and traveled extensively

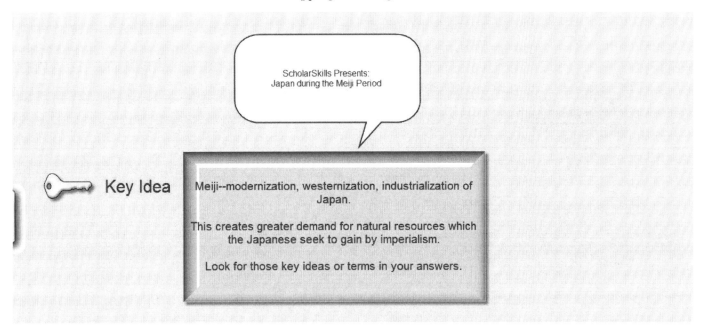

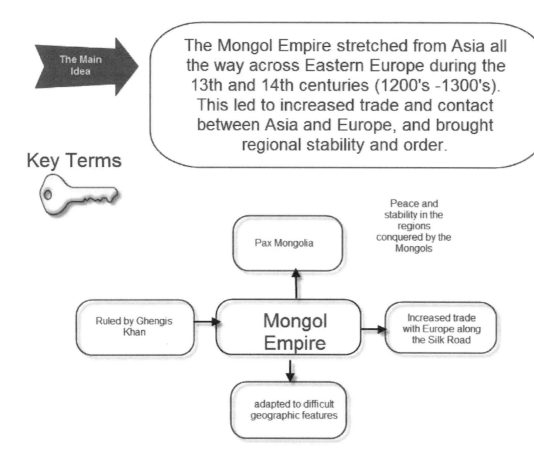

The Main
Idea

The Mongol Empire stretched from Asia all
the way across Eastern Europe during the
13th and 14th centuries (1200's -1300's).
This led to increased trade and contact
between Asia and Europe, and brought
regional stability and order.

Key Terms

Pax Mongolia

Peace and
stability in the
regions
conquered by the
Mongols

Ruled by Ghengis
Khan

Mongol
Empire

Increased trade
with Europe along
the Silk Road

adapted to difficult
geographic features

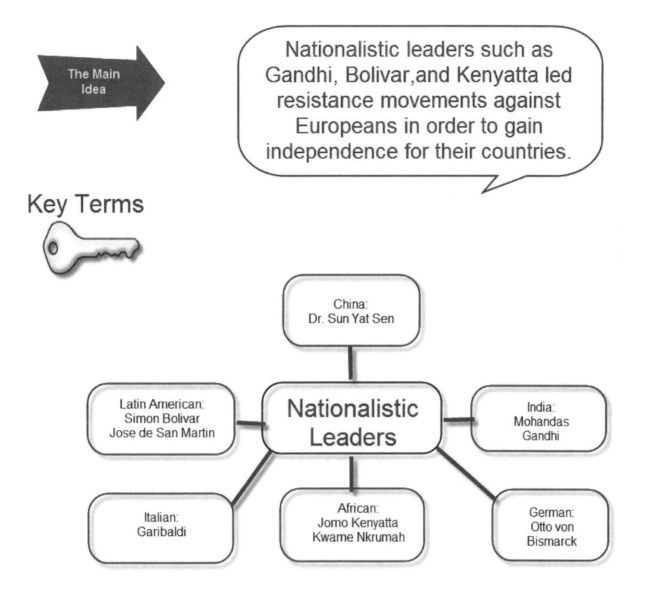

The Main Idea

Nationalistic leaders such as Gandhi, Bolivar, and Kenyatta led resistance movements against Europeans in order to gain independence for their countries.

Key Terms

China: Dr. Sun Yat Sen

Latin American: Simon Bolivar Jose de San Martin

Nationalistic Leaders

India: Mohandas Gandhi

Italian: Garibaldi

African: Jomo Kenyatta Kwame Nkrumah

German: Otto von Bismarck

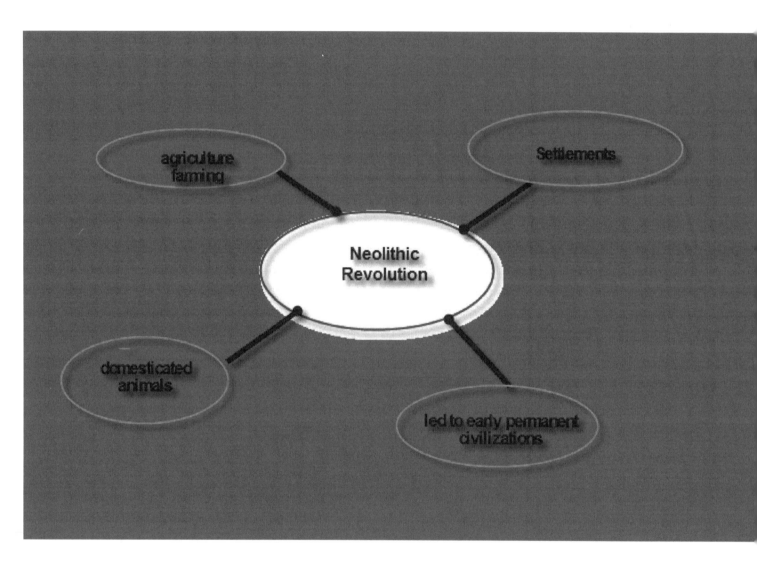

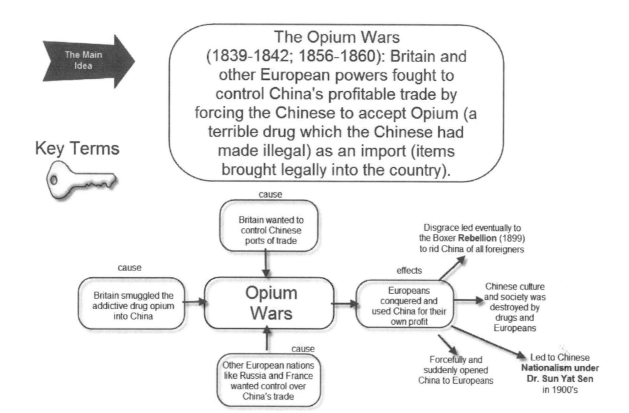

The Main Idea

The Opium Wars (1839-1842; 1856-1860): Britain and other European powers fought to control China's profitable trade by forcing the Chinese to accept Opium (a terrible drug which the Chinese had made illegal) as an import (items brought legally into the country).

Key Terms

cause

Britain wanted to control Chinese ports of trade

cause

Britain smuggled the addictive drug opium into China

Opium Wars

cause

Other European nations like Russia and France wanted control over China's trade

effects

Europeans conquered and used China for their own profit

Disgrace led eventually to the Boxer **Rebellion** (1899) to rid China of all foreigners

Chinese culture and society was destroyed by drugs and Europeans

Forcefully and suddenly opened China to Europeans

Led to Chinese **Nationalism under Dr. Sun Yat Sen** in 1900's

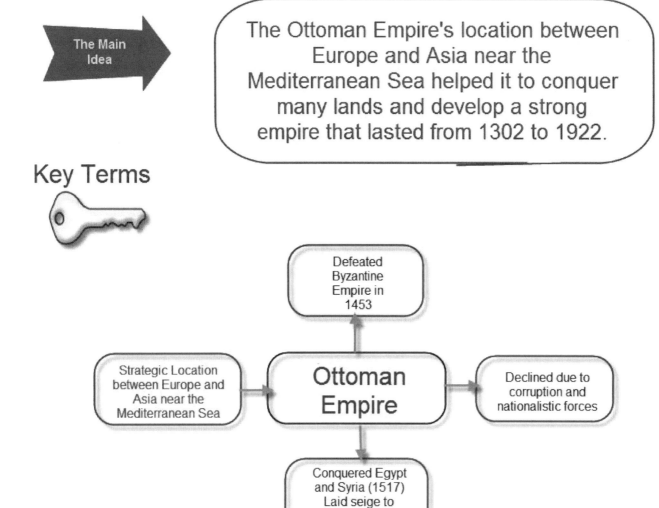

The Main Idea

The Ottoman Empire's location between Europe and Asia near the Mediterranean Sea helped it to conquer many lands and develop a strong empire that lasted from 1302 to 1922.

Key Terms

Defeated Byzantine Empire in 1453

Strategic Location between Europe and Asia near the Mediterranean Sea

Ottoman Empire

Declined due to corruption and nationalistic forces

Conquered Egypt and Syria (1517) Laid seige to Vienna (1529)

The Main Idea

Many great reformers throughout history have tried to bring about social, economic, and political changes that they thought were beneficial to their nations.

Key Terms

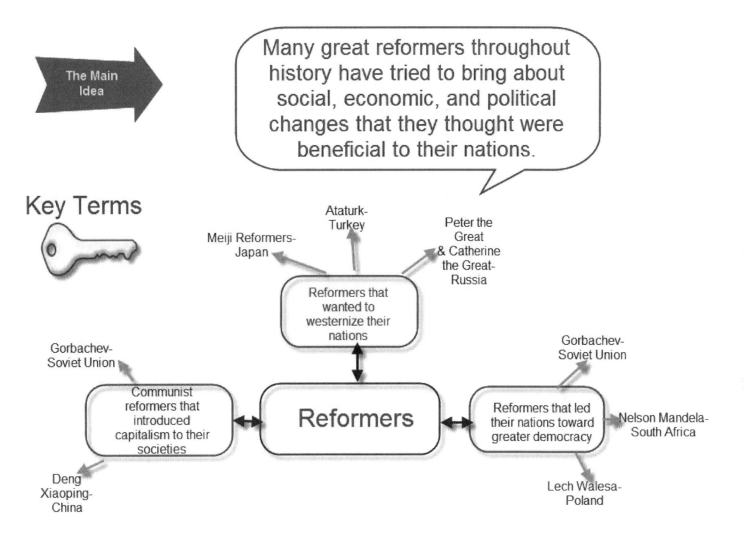

Ataturk-Turkey

Meiji Reformers-Japan

Peter the Great & Catherine the Great-Russia

Reformers that wanted to westernize their nations

Gorbachev-Soviet Union

Communist reformers that introduced capitalism to their societies

Deng Xiaoping-China

Reformers

Gorbachev-Soviet Union

Reformers that led their nations toward greater democracy

Nelson Mandela-South Africa

Lech Walesa-Poland

The Main
Idea

Key Terms

The Reformation:
Martin Luther opposed Roman
Catholic traditions such as the selling
of indulgences. The Pope rejected
Luther's arguments. This led to the
splitting of the Church into the Roman
Catholic and Protestant churches.
Religious unity had ended.

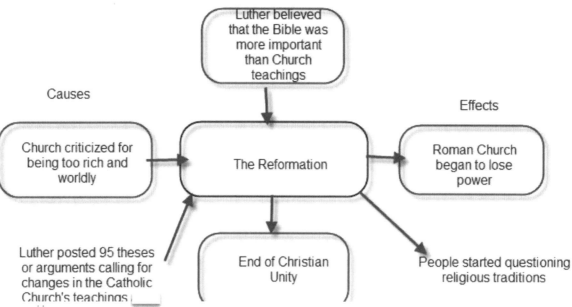

Luther believed that the Bible was more important than Church teachings

Causes

Effects

Church criticized for being too rich and worldly

The Reformation

Roman Church began to lose power

Luther posted 95 theses or arguments calling for changes in the Catholic Church's teachings

End of Christian Unity

People started questioning religious traditions

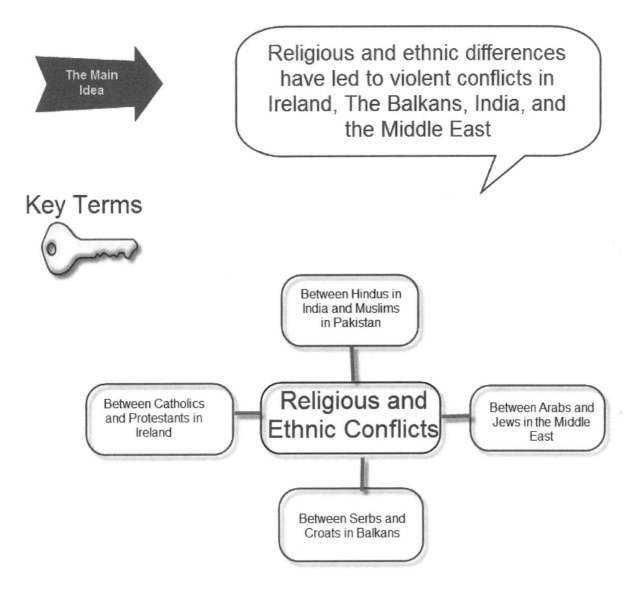

The Main Idea

Religious and ethnic differences have led to violent conflicts in Ireland, The Balkans, India, and the Middle East

Key Terms

Between Hindus in India and Muslims in Pakistan

Between Catholics and Protestants in Ireland

Religious and Ethnic Conflicts

Between Arabs and Jews in the Middle East

Between Serbs and Croats in Balkans

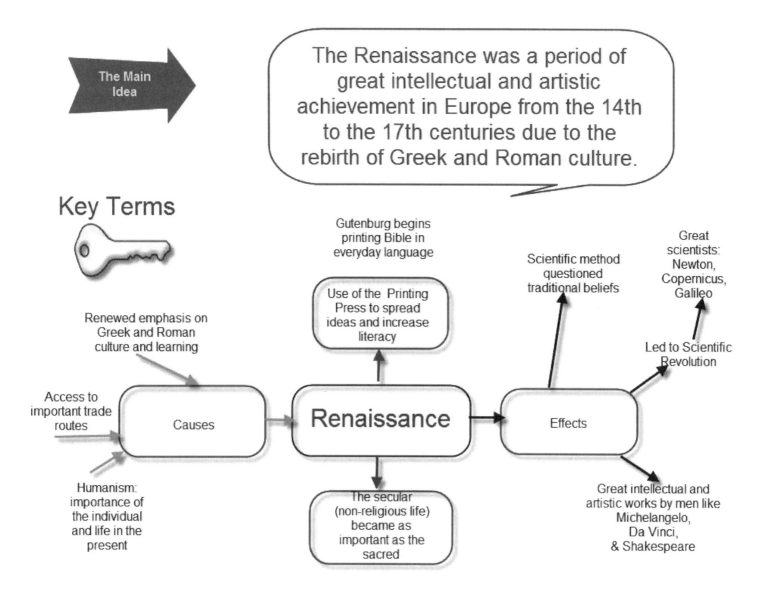

The Main Idea

The Renaissance was a period of great intellectual and artistic achievement in Europe from the 14th to the 17th centuries due to the rebirth of Greek and Roman culture.

Key Terms

Renewed emphasis on Greek and Roman culture and learning

Access to important trade routes

Humanism: importance of the individual and life in the present

Causes

Gutenburg begins printing Bible in everyday language

Use of the Printing Press to spread ideas and increase literacy

Renaissance

The secular (non-religious life) became as important as the sacred

Scientific method questioned traditional beliefs

Great scientists: Newton, Copernicus, Galileo

Led to Scientific Revolution

Effects

Great intellectual and artistic works by men like Michelangelo, Da Vinci, & Shakespeare

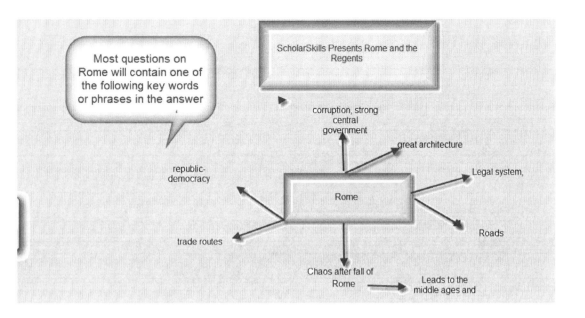

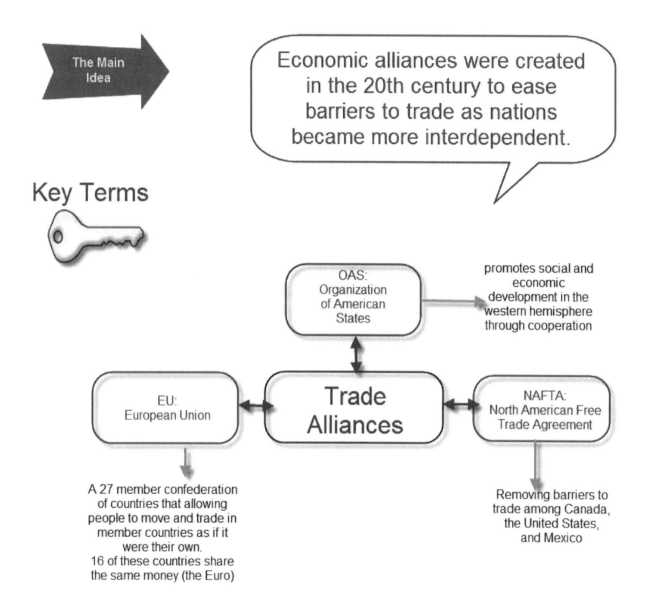

The Main Idea

Economic alliances were created in the 20th century to ease barriers to trade as nations became more interdependent.

Key Terms

OAS:
Organization of American States

promotes social and economic development in the western hemisphere through cooperation

Trade Alliances

EU:
European Union

NAFTA:
North American Free Trade Agreement

A 27 member confederation of countries that allowing people to move and trade in member countries as if it were their own.
16 of these countries share the same money (the Euro)

Removing barriers to trade among Canada, the United States, and Mexico

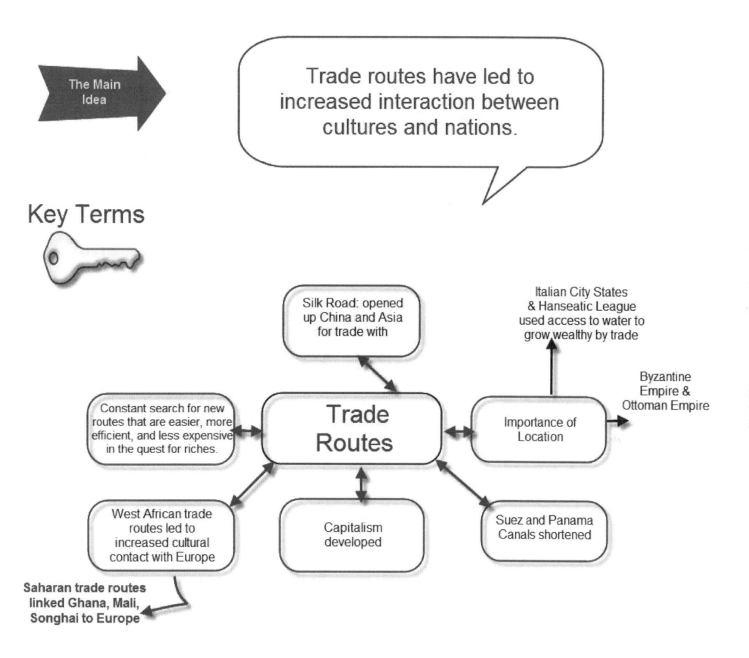

The Main Idea

Trade routes have led to increased interaction between cultures and nations.

Key Terms

Silk Road: opened up China and Asia for trade with

Italian City States & Hanseatic League used access to water to grow wealthy by trade

Constant search for new routes that are easier, more efficient, and less expensive in the quest for riches.

Trade Routes

Importance of Location

Byzantine Empire & Ottoman Empire

West African trade routes led to increased cultural contact with Europe

Capitalism developed

Suez and Panama Canals shortened

Saharan trade routes linked Ghana, Mali, Songhai to Europe

The Main Idea

Traditional societies: are usually agricultural communities that farm only enough for their families or villages and believe in keeping things the way that they have always been.

Key Terms

dependent upon the natural environment

Bartering: exchange of goods and services for goods and services

Traditional Societies

subsistence farming: only enough for food for families and village

change is rejected or comes very slowly

The Main Idea

The Triangular Trade: England ships traded manufactured goods to Africans in return for slaves. Then the ships would deliver slaves to the American South and to the West Indies for the money that they would later use to buy raw materials to transport back to England.

Key Terms

English ships trade goods for slaves

English Ships travel with manufactured goods to Africa

Ships return to England with manufactured goods

Slaves sold to West Indies and America

Triangular Trade

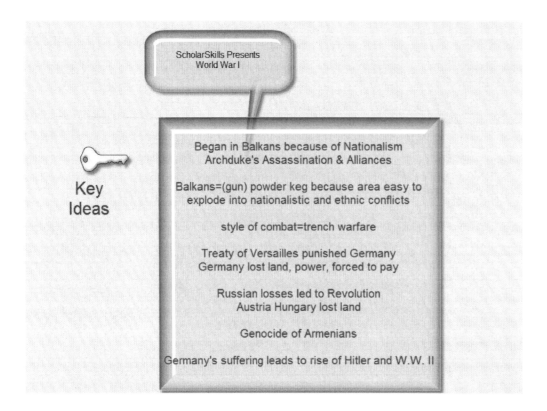

ScholarSkills Presents
World War I

Key
Ideas

Began in Balkans because of Nationalism
Archduke's Assassination & Alliances

Balkans=(gun) powder keg because area easy to
explode into nationalistic and ethnic conflicts

style of combat=trench warfare

Treaty of Versailles punished Germany
Germany lost land, power, forced to pay

Russian losses led to Revolution
Austria Hungary lost land

Genocide of Armenians

Germany's suffering leads to rise of Hitler and W.W. II

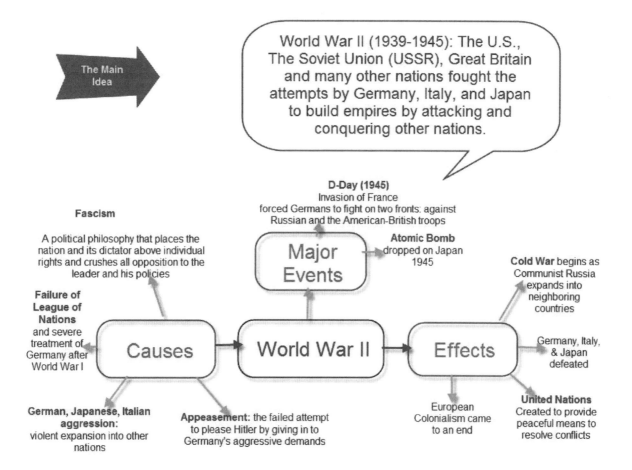

The Main Idea

World War II (1939-1945): The U.S., The Soviet Union (USSR), Great Britain and many other nations fought the attempts by Germany, Italy, and Japan to build empires by attacking and conquering other nations.

Fascism

A political philosophy that places the nation and its dictator above individual rights and crushes all opposition to the leader and his policies

Failure of League of Nations
and severe treatment of Germany after World War I

German, Japanese, Italian aggression:
violent expansion into other nations

Appeasement: the failed attempt to please Hitler by giving in to Germany's aggressive demands

D-Day (1945)
Invasion of France forced Germans to fight on two fronts: against Russian and the American-British troops

Atomic Bomb
dropped on Japan 1945

Major Events

Causes

World War II

Effects

Cold War begins as Communist Russia expands into neighboring countries

Germany, Italy, & Japan defeated

European Colonialism came to an end

United Nations
Created to provide peaceful means to resolve conflicts

The Main Idea

Zheng He was a 15th century Chinese explorer who sailed to promote trade and to collect wealth for his country. His travels proved that the Ming dynasty had advanced navigational technology.

Made in the USA
Middletown, DE
18 September 2015